I0814149

Lady Sunrise

Lady Sunrise

Marjorie Chan 陳以珏

Playwrights Canada Press
Toronto

For professional or amateur production rights, please contact:
Ian Arnold at Catalyst TCM
15 Old Primrose Lane, Toronto, ON M5A 4T1
416.568.8673 | ian@catalysttcm.com

LIBRARY AND ARCHIVES CANADA CATALOGUING IN PUBLICATION
Title: Lady sunrise / Marjorie Chan.
Names: Chan, Marjorie, author.
Description: A play.
Identifiers: Canadiana (print) 20220168962 | Canadiana (ebook) 20220168997 | ISBN 9780369103543 (softcover) | ISBN 9780369103567 (PDF) | ISBN 9780369103550 (HTML)
Classification: LCC PS8605.H355 L33 2022 | DDC C812/.6—dc23

Playwrights Canada Press operates on land which is the ancestral home of the Anishinaabe Nations (Ojibwe / Chippewa, Odawa, Potawatomi, Algonquin, Saulteaux, Nipissing, and Mississauga), the Wendat, and the members of the Haudenosaunee Confederacy (Mohawk, Oneida, Onondaga, Cayuga, Seneca, and Tuscarora), as well as Metis and Inuit peoples. It always was and always will be Indigenous land.

We acknowledge the financial support of the Canada Council for the Arts, the Ontario Arts Council (OAC), Ontario Creates, and the Government of Canada for our publishing activities.

Canada Council for the Arts | Conseil des arts du Canada

ONTARIO ARTS COUNCIL
CONSEIL DES ARTS DE L'ONTARIO
an Ontario government agency
un organisme du gouvernement de l'Ontario

Foreword

by Nina Lee Aquino

I saw *China Doll* in 2004 and from that moment I was chasing my chance to direct a Marjorie Chan play. I came close while I was still the artistic director of Cahoots Theatre—we were developing Marjorie's beautiful play *Hello Cello, Goodbye Heart*. And then when I (unexpectedly) became the artistic director of Factory Theatre in 2013, I was delighted and relieved that Marjorie still wanted to continue developing the play with me at Factory, under the new title *The Year of the Cello*.

However, it was simply not meant to be. We had devoted time to a couple of workshops over two years to develop the play, but something wasn't quite clicking and we decided to put the process on pause. I've had enough experience to know that this can sometimes happen at any given point in the development of a new play—even when you're working with one of the best playwrights out there, and, in my case, one of my favourite playwrights.

Of course, the realization that *The Year of the Cello* was not going to be *the* Marjorie Chan play Factory produced came just days *before* the workshop that had been set up for it in June 2018. Not wanting to pull the plug just yet on the allotted workshop funds and time that we had for Marjorie, she asked us if we wanted to look at another play of hers that had been metaphorically "sitting inside her drawer" for quite some time now. It had been commissioned and initially developed by the University of British Columbia and then subsequently developed by a handful of other theatre companies and play development centres. I don't remember the exact sequence of events after that proposal—whether company dramaturg Matt McGeachy read the draft and supported the idea to give this play a workshop or if I just immediately said, "Yes, let's do it"—without really knowing much about the play or that it required six actors—double the size of our aforementioned workshop!

All I knew was that as soon as I heard the first line of the play read aloud: "There are so many things that I believe in . . . " I was hooked.

Scene after scene, as the pages were turning, I fell more and more in love with the characters and the maze-like world(s) they inhabited. The image of a Chinese puzzle box kept appearing and reappearing in my mind's eye as the women of the play—a second-rate beauty queen, a wealthy condo developer, a ruthless bank executive, a madam, a blackjack dealer, and a trafficked sex worker—were all trapped in a container . . . with no exit. Each of these characters seem content to be on their destined paths, but, as the story unfolds, we realize that each is on a secret quest (whether they want to admit it or not) to get the hell out. Because underneath the luxury of the condos and casinos, the armour of opulence and power, we discover that everything and everyone is rotting inside. Broken, damaged, and tired by the weight of their self-made universes.

I saw characters dripping in pearls, bathed in shiny neon lights, heard the clicking of expensive high heels and felt the lush green of a blackjack table all juxtaposed against the backdrop of empty fake Prada purses, dirty bowls of leftover ramen, liquor glasses stained with lip gloss, and ashtrays filled with cigarette butts. And prescription pills. Lots and lots of prescription pills.

I loved how rich, nuanced, and multi-faceted the characters were, but, more importantly, how flawed they all were. I loved how Marjorie—playing with the common Asian icons of the "unhappy working-class immigrant" or "ultra-wealthy leisure dragon ladies"—was cutting through each of these characters with a sharp knife, like a surgeon—precise, brutal, and honest. If the characters appeared to be submissive or generous or subservient or funny (because by god, some of these characters have hilarious moments!), it was all a strategy to survive and thrive in their *Hunger Games*–like world.

I must admit that throughout the workshop my director brain could not shut off. The form of the play, although deceptively simple and presented mostly through a series of monologues, presented me as a director the most complex playground yet. The desire for each woman to hold their own space and present themselves to us beautifully butted up against the desire to connect these characters during the in-between moments. And maybe it was just my own directorial delusions of how I envision the ebb and flow of the piece, but I started seeing the invisible strings that Marjorie—consciously or subconsciously—masterfully tied to each and every one of the characters. My job, if I was given the chance to direct this piece (I hadn't asked her yet and didn't want to be presumptuous), was to create the webs that connect them all directly and indirectly. *Lady Sunrise* truly was a gift for *any* director to take on.

I didn't even need to get to the end of the reading to know that we were going to produce this at Factory. Not just *someday*, but *soon*.

I let Marjorie know our desire to see this on the Factory Mainstage. I remember her crying from joy and us squealing with glee that we finally found "the one" that Factory would have the privilege of premiering. That same day, after the workshop, after the initial tears and laughter of confirming our interest in her play, I asked—with all the courage I could muster—if Marjorie would consider me to direct the production. BUT only if she thought I was the right one. She looked at me, puzzled, and lovingly yelled (only the way Marjorie can), "Of course I want you to direct the production, silly! Why the hell would you even ask me that?!?! It's all yours, my friend." And it was my turn to cry in front of her, speechless and full of gratitude and excitement. Finally, finally, finally.

Lady Sunrise had its world premiere as part of our fiftieth anniversary season in February 2020, a year after that initial workshop reading. Each production in the fiftieth season paid tribute to one of Factory's past artistic directors—this was the production that honoured my artistry, and I was so grateful it was written by the one playwright I had been chasing for almost fifteen years.

With a string of firsts in Asian Canadian theatre, Nina was the founding artistic director of fu-GEN Asian Canadian Theatre Company in 2002, organized the first Asian Canadian theatre conference, edited the first (two-volume) Asian Canadian play anthology Love + Relasianships, *and co-edited the first (award-winning) book on Asian Canadian theatre. She became artistic director of Cahoots Theatre in 2009, Factory Theatre in 2012, and the National Arts Centre English Theatre in September 2022. Awards for her work include the Ken McDougall Award, the Canada Council for the Arts John Hirsch Prize, the Toronto Theatre Critics Awards for Best Director, Toronto Arts Foundation Margo Bindhart and Rita Davies Cultural Leadership Award, and three Dora Awards for Outstanding Direction.*

Preface

In 2012 I was approached by Dr. Siyuan (Steven) Liu of the University of British Columbia and director John Cooper to see if I would be interested in doing a "cleanup" of Cao Yu's famous 1936 play *Sunrise*, in order to make it more stageable in the modern day. I had never heard of this play or this playwright. Cao Yu was inspired by the naturalistic styles of Anton Chekhov and Henrik Ibsen, uncommon in China at that time. The play itself I found to be expansive, and funny, and tragic. After reading it, I declined the commission as described.

But I had a different proposal. I asked, instead of pulling merely the language forward, if I could pull the *characters* forward and extrapolate their existence in a contemporary context. The female protagonists of Cao Yu's play resonated with me, and my imagination leapt easily to wonder about who their modern-day counterparts might be. I began a framework of writing about these Asian women in Vancouver and Richmond, adding a few more to round out the narrative. In form I wanted to give these characters the fullest of stages and the time to speak, in all of their contrariness and complexities. Over the years, *Lady Sunrise* found her own rhythm and purpose.

There is an intransigent consumerism that has driven most of Hong Kong's colonial history. The narrative is that Hong Kong was "only" a fishing village before a British flag was planted, which brought international commerce. (The truth is that trade was always present in the region.) Indeed, the '80s in Hong Kong was a bastion of excess, with transient foreigners touching down to make money before jetting home.

The '90s had the feeling of *fin de siècle*, a lean in to decadence as the countdown for a return to China loomed. The 2000s saw the beginning of a sobering while people desperately tried to hang onto unsustainable lifestyles. For *Lady Sunrise*, this serves as the historical background for these six diasporic women, all on the precipice of change. Money equals power, and all the women struggle with their relationship to it and its ultimate cost.

Thank you for making time for these women.

Marjorie Chan 陳以珏
April 2022

Inspired by Cao Yu's *Sunrise* and originally commissioned by the University of British Columbia, with development support from the University of British Columbia, the Banff Playwrights Lab, Cahoots Theatre, the Arts Club Theatre Company, Factory Theatre, the Ontario Arts Council, and the Wuchien Michael Than Foundation, *Lady Sunrise* was first produced by Factory Theatre, Toronto, from February 15–March 8, 2020, with the following cast and creative team:

Sherry: Belinda Corpuz
Auntie Ku: Ma-Anne Dionisio
Dealer Li: Zoé Doyle
Banker Wong: Rosie Simon
Penny: Lindsay Wu
Charmaine: Louisa Zhu

Director: Nina Lee Aquino
Set Design: Camellia Koo
Costume Design: Jackie Chau
Lighting Design: Michelle Ramsay
Sound Design and Composition: Debashis Sinha
Dramaturg: Matt McGeachy
Assistant Director and Movement Director: Natasha Mumba
Apprentice Lighting Designer: Ella Wiechowski
Production Manager: Alanna McConnell
Stage Manager: Tamara Protic
Apprentice Stage Manager: Hannah MacMillan
Head of Props: Vanessa Janiszewski
Head of Wardrobe: Joyce Padua
Fight Director: Louisa Zhu
Scenic Artist: Dan Jakobi
Carpenters: Clint Bouwman and Dalton Villeneuve-Marini

Characters

Penny, also known as Lulu
A Chinese Canadian woman, born in Canada, with family from Hong Kong, fluent in both cultures. A bon vivant girl in "entertainment." Charming, sweet.

Sherry, also known as the Girl or the Shrimp
A young teenage girl from Southeast Asia, trafficked for sex work. She is tiny but strong.

Tawny Ku, also known as Auntie Ku
An older, wealthy Hong Kong expat, who lives life to the fullest. She is larger than life.

Banker Wong, also known as Vivian
A middle-aged Chinese Canadian woman, and a high-up executive. She is ambitious and cold.

Dealer Li, also known as Li Wang
A middle-aged Chinese woman who works at the casino. She is compassionate but tired.

Charmaine, also known as Auntie or the Mouse or the Monkey
A middle-aged Asian or Southeast Asian woman who manages a "massage parlour." She is pragmatic.

Notes

Set in and around Richmond and Vancouver, British Columbia, over the course of a week in the fall of 2009. The prologue, epilogue, and snapshots/images are out of time from the overall chronology. In considering the staging, a sense of ensemble is important.

The characters spend a lot of time alone in their lives. They talk. They talk a lot. They are perhaps not to be trusted, and are often not truthful. They perhaps need to just hear themselves.

As well, as indicated above, all the characters have two names or more, representing the multiple identities they present to the world. The clearest example is the dichotomy of the very public, confident "Lulu" and the very personal, vulnerable "Penny." I would encourage actors to consider the identity their character may be choosing to present from scene to scene.

In several scenes, Penny appears as a memory, and is not physically present in the action of the scene. Often, these interjections represent a more truthful version of events. These sections are indicated with italicized text.

A vertical bar (|) appearing within a line of dialogue indicates alternative dialogue for that character. This primarily concerns characters where there is fluidity in the casting that will result in subtle differences due to ethnicity or language spoken.

Prologue

Images of PENNY *at the Sunrise pageant.*

PENNY: *(as if answering a question at the pageant)* There are so many things that I believe in. But most of all, what I want to tell young women, the young women of today, is to believe in yourself.

I believe that women can do anything. We can do anything. Times have changed. We just have to imagine it. Dream.

I hope one day my daughters and granddaughters will look at me and say, her, her, HER?

She is my hero.

So that is why, why we—to, to work together—and to depend on each other, but mostly believe in ourselves. And that is how we will win, how we fight against the . . . pat-tree-archie.[1]

My name is Lulu and I'm from Richmond, British Columbia, Canada.

She repeats this in Cantonese if possible.

And I want to be your MISS SUNRISE 2005!

---

1 E.g., some mangled pronunciation.

Scene 1: Penthouse

Years later. PENNY *is in a luxury apartment. She is putting on lip gloss.*

PENNY: Can you be addicted to lip gloss?
You have to keep putting it on. Like all the time.
It's shiny, sure, but it never sticks.

She smacks her lips.

I have no idea why, but my lips are like crazy dry all the time.
It must be, y'know, the altitude, like, penthouse, that's pretty high, right?
I was supposed to go to this hoity-toity thing, a gala.
Auntie wanted me to go, right?
Back in the day, like waaaaaaay back, like the '80s, when y'know making money was real easy, Auntie was really popular.
And not to be mean or anything, but it has been a long time since she was a looker. But—she's still on these invite lists, cuz guess what?
She's rrrrrrrrrrrich. Like stinking, pee-yew, roll your Rs rich.

Anyway, she's the best. She's not like my real auntie, like for blood. It's more like she's my friend, like best friends who do everything together! Who shop together, go to dim sum together, and get our nails done together!

She looks at her nails.

Ugh. Don't look at my nails. They look like trash, like I pick fruit or raise goats or something for a living. Gross.

Okay so Auntie wants me to go to this fancy thing tonight, right?

She wants me to meet "other" people. She wants me to date someone "nice." Like omigod. OMG. I can get my own dates!

At one point, I made a decision.
For my own sanity and for how I want to live, right?
I made a decision—I have to date a certain kind of guy.

So, this was a couple years ago—there was this "nice" guy, who I knew back in high school, so like I hadn't seen him since forever.

Like before the pageants stuff, before Hong Kong, so like so long ago.
Like, my last pageant win was like almost five years ago.
So this guy, outta nowhere, he like finds me online and sends me a DM, okay? "I want to see you. You look amazing," et cetera, right?

So, I'm like, okay, come to the club with me tonight?
It's a fashion thing! It will be fierce, I say.
And then he's like, "But I want to see you, not hang out in a club!"
He's so dumb. Like this thing is open bar.
I mean come on, O-PEN BAAAR!!
I wasn't going to miss it.
So, we're there, right?
I offer him a drink—he didn't want it, fine.
I wanted to dance, and he wanted to sit, okay!
I said, "Let's make out," and he takes my hand and says, "Let's talk!"

Talk!?

She laughs.

Amazing, right? So, fine, we're gonna head back here. He's driving, but I reach over his lap to touch him. He swats my hand away! A total tease.

Then we get here, and I'm like, okay, maybe now we'll make out? Instead, he pulls out this book. I mean, it's a real book, like a real published book, but it's small. Because get this. It's POETRY. His poetry. Worse, here's the worst part—inside, he's signed it. Hahaha. He signed it, "For Penny." First of all, that's not my name anymore, that's my old name. And then second of all, he says, "Penny for your thoughts?" Like I have never heard that before. And third of all, why do we even have pennies anymore anyway, they're not worth anything!

... I mean yah, in high school, we did have a thing. The kinda thing teenagers have ... writing each other love notes kinda thing, making out, staying up all night laughing, whatever. We were just kids. I had the pageants and modelling. So, so ... I was busy. Back and forth to Hong Kong, the whole thing. No way I was going to stick with him. No way.

Beat.

His name's Tom, but I called him Tommmmmyyyyyy. He would say, "Whaaaaaaa-aaaaat????" And I would say again, "Tommmmmmmyyyyy," and he would say, "Whaaaaaa-aaaaaat?" and we would just go back and forth. Tommmy—Whaaaat? Tommmy—Whaaaaat?[2] until we were just laughing. For no reason. Silly.

...

Anyway. I don't know how much a "poet" makes, but I'm pretty sure that it's not enough. So anyway, when he gave me that book, that's when I made the decision. About who I date, y'know. I gotta look out for myself because no one else will.

---

2 Or more times if needed.

I guess I could've gone out with Auntie tonight. It would have made her happy . . . but for real . . . I read, like, I think fashion people will be there . . . And that crowd, that modelling crowd, and has-been photographers . . . You know what they say about photographers, right? They're only as good as their last girl!

But seriously, anyway, what would I wear?

She laughs. Her phone buzzes. She looks at the number.

Oh for Chrissakes! I don't have it! Go the fuck away!

She throws the phone and puts her head in her hands.

Scene 2: Vancouver City Hall

Everything that AUNTIE KU *does is big, her wardrobe and personality are no exception.*

AUNTIE KU: An investment! Plain and simple!

I have the money, why shouldn't I be able to buy what I want? What does it matter if I live here, or in Hong Kong, or wherever? What does it matter if I leave it empty or not? It's my money. And if I want to buy property, if I want to buy a condo, a whole tower of condos, why shouldn't I be allowed to?

Do I care about buildings? Do I care about alleviating density in the city? Do I care about multi-use assets?

Heavens, no. Not a bit.

But I know how to say the right things. I will charm the pants off this city councillor until he begs me to build in his riding. You watch how fast the permits get approved after I'm through with him, yesiree. A new deal, new condos, and I. Am. In. I can't tell you which ones—but here's a hint—only the hottest address in Vancouver! The permits—are just a technicality…

If we break ground before the end of this month, put everyone on double shifts, this baby could be up before the Olympics.

I know what you are thinking…

"Not the deal with Frankie Pan? Not those condos, right? He has been trotting that deal up and down the block without any luck."

Okay. Maybe he did some bad deals in the past, but he seems okay. Lulu and him are ... friends. He's the one that put all the pieces together. I'm sure, I'm sure it's fine.

PENNY appears as a memory, not actually in the scene.

PENNY: *What do you mean? We're friends! So he helps me out every once in a while—that's what friends are for!*

AUNTIE KU: I think in the end the deal will be all right. As long as the financing ...

What's life without a little risk? The good thing is Penny finally showed some interest in business because of Frankie! I was hoping that if I came on board she could shadow me and learn a bit. And maybe I could lend her something later off the interest and she could start her own investing, y'know?

But I had no idea that she was so hopeless ... I don't know how she's been living all these years ...

PENNY: *Thank you so much, Auntie! You saved my life! You don't know how long I've been wanting this!*

AUNTIE KU: A few months ago, I tried to introduce her to my banker, thinking, hoping, she could get a handle on her finances ... Penny—I mean Lulu. She hates that I call her Penny sometimes. So, Lulu is bright, she could do this! She just has to want to. I've tried so hard to get it through her hairsprayed head! Of course, it's easier to let other people handle everything, but you have to know what's going on. You have to keep your eye on your money. Everyone is out for something, and if they can steal it from you, they will.

PENNY: *Auntie! How many times do I have to tell you! He doesn't want anything! You're so old fashioned!*

AUNTIE KU: Penny convinced me Frankie Pan could be trusted. I trust Penny . . .
Well, I've committed my portion already, so, so not worth fretting about it now . . . The things I do . . .

She's not my daughter, but she's actually so much more like me—SO MUCH more like me. I can't help but want to look out for her. My real daughter, well, she, she, she can take care of herself, what, with her career in not-for-profit, can you believe it, and her, her . . . partner. They have a kid. Don't ask me, I don't even want to know how. They're in Toronto, of course. What a dreadful, dreary place. Too busy to call . . . My daughter doesn't need me, obviously! Or she would call!

Now Penny . . . I've tried to swing her something—anything, a gossip show, or a bit of hosting. I've tried, I've tried before but . . . after her "thing" . . . This line of work, this kind of work, it's not hard but . . . you do have to show up and be reliable!

It's not like she ever really tried to get a regular job . . . I mean, it is one thing to have fun with some men. Trust me, men can be fun—let them buy you a few drinks and a bauble or two.

But then, once they start to pay, pay for bigger things, big trips, furs, rent . . . How much do you have to buy before you own?

Her phone rings.

My banker ... Vivian. Gotta take this!

(answering) Luck and Grace Industries! CEO Tawny Ku speaking, please tell me you're going to say yes?

Scene 3: Head Bank Branch, Vancouver

BANKER WONG is in a boxy suit. Blunt hair. No nonsense. Grey.

BANKER WONG: Crazy Ku is what we call her around here. That's not her real name of course. Crazy Ku has made me a lot of money over the years, which I appreciate. Trust me, I appreciate it.

At the end of this quarter, I, me, Vivian Wong, will be personally responsible for bringing in a third of the pre-tax revenue here at this bank. The leading bank in Canada—but you knew that! Eight straight quarters, I've led this bank in net growth. That isn't chicken feed. That kind of revenue is tied to a big fat bonus, and when I say fat, I do mean fat, plus a few extra weeks of vacation. But let's face it, it's better to have the money than the vacation time. What am I going to do with accrued vacation time when I'm dead?

She pauses. She didn't mean to say "dead." She sips water or distracts herself for a second.

Course, it still is a tricky time. You don't want to get cocky just because the papers are telling you how rosy it is. Could it happen again? Oh, there could always be another crash, crisis, collapse. There could be a correction right round the corner. It takes guts to steer through these storms. Takes nerves of steel, or balls of stone. Balls. Of. Stone. Tits of stone doesn't quite have the same ring, does it? Don't look at my tits.

But this deal, this deal of Crazy Ku's? It is a stinker. Don't get me wrong, I know risk. I understand risk. Here's an example. A deal, my deal fell through, twenty-six million out the window, in the blink of an eye. Whoosh. Okay. Wow. That one hurt, sure. But just for a second. Then I take a breath, recover, focus, what's the plan? What are we going to do about it? Don't panic. Don't freak out. Don't freak out. But think. Strategize. Plan. What action can we take to mitigate the damage? And once you know, once you have a plan—you do it. You go for it. Right away, no hesitation, confident—GO. That is why I play with the big boys.

Now Crazy Ku wishes she could play with the big boys. She wishes. She's a bit of a handful, that one. Smart but she has a tendency to be sloppy and trust the wrong people. Emotional decisions instead of reason. It'll probably get her in the end.

She's in a hell of lot better position than she used to be, I can tell you that. You should have seen her accounts when her husband first died.

Yikes. Everyone thought Mr. Luk was rich, filthy rich, but his accounts . . . We cleaned it up. We worked with her, advised, consolidated her debts, diversified her holdings, invested—cautiously, carefully. And eventually. Patiently. We built her wealth back. We built her back.

We built Tawny Ku.

But this new deal she's on? Why? Why would you invest with a builder like that? Same builder that failed all his certificates, that had all those leaky condos in the '90s. Same builder, different name. I mean, do your research.

Because seriously, if we get the big one, and everyone says Vancouver is due, if we do get the big earthquake? Then that building will end up a pile of rubble. Just a train wreck waiting to happen. No thank you. I wouldn't touch it with a ten-foot pole. I don't know where she'll get the rest of the money from, definitely not from us. Probably from some B lender.

I wash my hands of it. Not my circus, not my monkeys.

(leaning in to gossip) Thing is, Crazy Ku can't even take care of her own children. Cut her own daughter off... who knows why? I heard that it was because she didn't like the fact that her daughter is... well... I can't get behind that. Not that I've had the time to even think about that...

Not when there is money to be made!

So a while back, Tawny picks up this whippy little starlet, Peppy or something. Those Hong Kong pageants churn these girls out, like a factory. New one every year, looks exactly like the old one. And guess what, the older model is obsolete! Business model sound familiar to you?

Anyway, this girl, she's Crazy Ku's next project. Where the girl's real parents are, who the heck knows. So she brings Lala Skinny Minny in here a few months ago, to look at her "portfolio." This girl's non-existent "portfolio." No investments, no savings, no assets. But she did have her modelling portfolio with her, which she offered to show me. I declined. I mean. What is the point. What a waste of time.

I mean, an hour of time, an hour of my time, from an executive like me, can cost the bank millions of dollars.

I don't say that to brag, that's the truth.

Beat. An alarm sounds on her phone. She reaches for a bottle of pills and quickly takes one, dry.

Scene 4: Penthouse

PENNY *quickly takes a pill while her phone rings. She is dressed for going out to a club.*

She lets her phone ring.

PENNY: My friend Frankie! I call him Frankie 'cause he likes that. Tonight, he's taking me out to the club. Which will give me my chance to work it. And, oh, am I going to work it! *(looks at phone)* It's okay to let it ring a couple of times.

She takes a deep breath and answers, immediately chipper.

(on phone) Frankieeeeee! How are ya, baby? Are we going to hit the club or not?

…

Uh huh. Okay, but don't keep a young girl waiting! She won't wait around forever!

…

I'm just joking, oh my gawd! You know I love you, Frankie!!

She hangs up, frustrated.

Once upon time, like when I was younger, there is no way any man would've kept me waiting. Like for real. How rude, right?

Like, once upon a time . . .

Once you win one of those things, a pageant, you get noticed. They put your picture in the paper, you start to go to events, and eventually the next time they need a pretty girl to stand next to an ugly politician, they call you!

Success!

Anyway, I won one like five years ago—it got me back to Asia. And I did loads, and I mean loads of gigs, modelling, hosting, presenting. And it is a skill. It's not just about being pretty. Even though I am very pretty.[3]

But now, now I'm back. I mean, back in Canada.

Because I'm fat.

No, haha!

Because I'm old.

Just kidding.

How old am I? No, really, how old am I?

I'm just asking. People in Asia always guess too old. But here?

I dunno why. People in Canada, especially *(whispers)* white people, they always guess too young. Sometimes they guess crazy young!

---

3 She's joking. Or is she?

(re-enacts flirtatiously) How old am I? Oh my god, how could I be that young? Hahaha!

She playfully swats an imaginary suitor and rolls her eyes, then drops the act.

Seriously? How could I be in a club drinking Cristal[4] with them if I was that young?

I think that sometimes they wish, they wish—and when I say "they" I mean, you know what I mean: men of the male species. Men, right? Men, they want you to be that young.

Because they want to fuck you. They want to fuck a girl.

That is fucked up, right?

She laughs.

Like I know, I know Asian women, we look young. I can make my voice high—I know I'm girly. I like girly things. So what, I like Hello Kitty, I like sparkles, SO WHAT? I wear pink, SO FUCKING WHAT? It doesn't make me a girl—it doesn't make me a child. I'm a woman where it counts.

Beat.

I have all sorts of friends. Bankers, businessmen, civil servants, but mostly bankers. When I say bankers, I mean everyone in finance, stocks, trading, whatever—I just call them all bankers—it's all the same to me. The bankers are the closest to the money so . . . I do what I can to live,

---

4 Or whatever is outrageously expensive and hip to drink.

and so I enjoy the privileges of a woman.

Just because I dress nicely and treat men nicely, people assume. They make assumptions. Okay, so I flirt. Whatever, I'm just being friendly.

And if my friend wants to buy me a new handbag, who I am to say no?

She fetches the handbag.

There are only five hundred of these bad boys made in whole wide world. Five hundred, and I have one of them. Look at the stitching! You could use this bag for a hundred years and that stitching will not come undone. That's quality! That's what you're paying for!

Do you know at the end of the season? If they don't sell off the bags, they are basically worthless at that point! They're not worth anything anymore because the new one is coming out! So do you know what they do with the old purses? The company, somewhere off in China, BURNS them. They burn them! Isn't that crazy? They just put them in a pile and light them on fire! I mean, these things go for a lot. I mean easily five grand! Mine is worth five grand. Imagine all those beautiful purses, these expensive purses, burning. Burn, burn, burn.

Beat.

I have seen lineups in Hong Kong, lineups up and down the street—you would not believe—to get the latest handbag! Like, so many people. Like, the whole street filled.

...

You know what they say about Hong Kong, right? If you can't make it in

Hong Kong, well, you can just throw yourself into the harbour! Or get crushed by a train! In Hong Kong, they've got some fantastic, tall buildings, and they say the view on the way down is spectacular!

That's what they say.

Not really.

There is no saying about what happens if you don't make it in Hong Kong. Because in Hong Kong, not making it is not an option.

> PENNY *attaches a fascinator or some other shiny thing. Now she's ready for the club.*

Scene 5: Sidewalk Outside of a Club

Late at night. SHERRY *is swirling a jewelled fascinator, a trophy. She is tiny but fierce.*

SHERRY: I got from her.
So fast, she didn't see.
Didn't care, maybe.
Maybe she so much, she don't care. Maybe she has so much, she don't care.

I see her, you understand?
I see her, I know she go from club there, her home there.
On top floor, very top I am sure.
She live so high.
Late night I know, I see her.
Car come at night, I see her get out.
Different man, but they're polite.
Hold her hand.
So nice.
Nice man.
Rich man.

I see her.
I see her every day.
From massage place, back window.
I can see.
No one around see me, but I see.

I see her,
I think

Give me.
I see her hair, so pretty, someone fix it, yes?
Give me, I think.
I see her I think,
Why can I no have this? | Why can't I have this?

These things she has,
These things I want:
Rings, and shoes, and sometime fur,
White fur, so clean like—

I want, she have; she have but I want, do you understand?

Cars, taxis all night at night come home,
Car because she come home so late at night, you know?
So very late.
But tonight—
I see her,
See her leaving club.
No car, you understand,
Walking, she's walking.
She's walking, I see her,
I follow, okay?

PENNY appears as a memory, not in the scene.

PENNY: *Excuse me.*

SHERRY: She not stop, just like this with her hand. | She doesn't stop, just like this with her hand.
Like I have camera or want autograph. | Like I have a camera or want an autograph.

No, I'm not a fan. Not a movie fan. Not me.
So I walk with her.
She walk faster.
I say, "Why you no take taxi?"
Take taxi. Why you no take taxi? | Take taxi. Why no taxi?

PENNY: *None of your business.*

SHERRY: I know, I see, she only take taxi when she has men.
Men who go to her, understand?

I say, "Where man? Where your man? No man tonight, lady?"

PENNY: *Go away.*

SHERRY: "I know," I say. "Teach me, show me.
You can do, show me.
I want to do different."

PENNY: *Leave me alone!*

SHERRY: I can do too.
Just lie on your back,
What I do,
Same,
Okay.

PENNY: *What?*

SHERRY: Only different.
Nice shoe,
Nice dress,

Otherwise same like me!

PENNY: *Shut the fuck up!*

SHERRY: I say,
"Help me, okay?
Help me, I don't come don't follow. | Help me, then I won't come, won't follow."

Help me.
Give me some nice clothes
Or some nice thing,
Some old thing you don't want.
You have extra,
You have more,
You have to help me.

You teach me.
I want to do like you,
Live like you.
Show me to be friends,
Friends with men
Who pay but don't hurt,
Who buy but don't take.

Show me how to do!

She stare at me, just stare.

I beg, okay? Okay, lady.
They are going to give me to a mean man.
They give me to him.

He's mean, so bad, everyone know this. | He's mean, so bad, everyone knows this.
Bad, bad man.
He pay, he pay a lot so they give me to him.
The man, he come and he say he want smallest, okay, me!
That's me!

He bad very bad… | He's bad, very bad…

She's so stupid. She stare. She say nothing. I get mad. | She's so stupid. She stare. She says nothing. I get mad.

She say nothing, make me so mad! | She says nothing, make me so mad!
NOTHING! SHE THINK NOTHING! I GET MAD! | NOTHING! SHE THINKS NOTHING! I GET MAD!

I scream, I scream!

Just give me, give me something! You have so much!
Give me something! Give to me, give to me!
I grab her bag, I grab her dress, I grab her hair,
I grab this thing, I grab to grab anything,
Anything I can, I grab, I grab, I grab, I GRAB!

I grab and I pull close, you know.
My face close to her
"Help me," I say.

Help me.

Beat.

Nothing. Nothing in her eyes, okay.

I see nothing, you understand?

I am not so much, not so strong, no family here.
But me?
Me?
But I am not nothing.
My eyes, can you see, still something!

I AM SOMETHING!

I take my hand off.

How can she be nothing?
She is all clean, and rich.
On TV. Many friends, many things.

But inside, in her eyes…

She dead. She dead already. | She's dead. She's dead already.
I can't see her.

Scene 6: Outside the Massage Parlour

Richmond. Too early for a run, and too late to still be awake. CHARMAINE *is on the sidewalk smoking, unseen. Along comes* BANKER WONG *in expensive workout attire. She pauses, out of breath—she has been pushing hard. She gets a cramp in her calf and needs to stop, leaning. All of a sudden* BANKER WONG *breaks into a violent, unnatural coughing fit. It is extended, unusual. She spits onto the sidewalk.*

CHARMAINE *watches her dispassionately and maybe even a little amused. (*CHARMAINE*'s first few lines could be in a language other than English if possible/desired, depending on casting.)* BANKER WONG *realizes that* CHARMAINE *has been watching.*

BANKER WONG: What are you looking at?

CHARMAINE: You.

BANKER WONG: What.

CHARMAINE: You a bit crazy, right?

They go back to ignoring each other. Finally:

(in English) You want me to fix?

BANKER WONG: I'm sorry?

CHARMAINE: I do it. Your leg, okay? I can fix.
Sure, I do massage, okay.

BANKER WONG raises her eyebrows, skeptical.

True.

CHARMAINE points behind her at the massage shop, but we don't see what she is pointing at.

BANKER WONG is even more skeptical.

What—you think I hurt you?

BANKER WONG: I didn't mean—

CHARMAINE: Oh boy, you a stupid lady. Just want to help you—but you don't want it.

BANKER WONG: Whatever.

CHARMAINE: You want to be in pain, you go on then. Me, I smoke.

Beat. BANKER WONG is still in pain from her charley horse.

BANKER WONG: Ahhhh . . .

CHARMAINE: Hmmmpf.

BANKER WONG: What?

CHARMAINE: Nothing.

Beat.

I do it, okay? I fix, I fix.

In a quick motion, CHARMAINE puts out her cigarette and begins to massage BANKER WONG's leg.

BANKER WONG: Hey . . . !

CHARMAINE: It no good?

BANKER WONG: Ow, no, no, it's good, ow.

CHARMAINE: You hard—you hard, you know.

BANKER WONG: Ow.

CHARMAINE: Why you working so hard?

BANKER WONG: I don't know.

CHARMAINE: Stupid—you work so hard.

BANKER WONG: I know.

Beat.

CHARMAINE: How much money you need anyway, no need to work so hard. You make lots of money?

CHARMAINE finds a particularly tender spot.

BANKER WONG: Owwwww!

CHARMAINE: You keep working so hard, you die soon! One day, you no get up and you die. Or worse, you live, you live but you want to die. You want to die all the time. That is worse.

Beat.

That's a joke.

BANKER WONG: It's not funny.

CHARMAINE: You not funny, that's your problem.

BANKER WONG: I am plenty funny. I make jokes all the time.

CHARMAINE: Sure.

BANKER WONG cracks a smile.

BANKER WONG: You don't believe me?

They both laugh a bit.

CHARMAINE: No! You crazy lady! You work too hard, not laugh.

Beat.

I know you know.

BANKER WONG: I know.

CHARMAINE: You live near here?

Guess must have good view, no? Very expensive.

BANKER WONG: I don't live near here. I ran here.

CHARMAINE: Huh.

CHARMAINE finishes her massage.

Okay, better, right?

BANKER WONG is suddenly overcome with emotion. She is exhausted. No one is ever nice to her or laughs with her.

BANKER WONG: . . .

CHARMAINE: Okay?

BANKER WONG: . . .

CHARMAINE: I hurt you?

Finally . . .

BANKER WONG: I'm sorry, I didn't mean to . . .

CHARMAINE: Work is work.

BANKER WONG: It's not my work. I'm good at my work.

CHARMAINE: . . . But you don't like it.
Oh. They don't think you are good.

BANKER WONG: No!
I don't know.
Does anyone like their work?
Do you?

CHARMAINE: . . . Work is work.

BANKER WONG: It's not my work.

I'm, I'm . . . going through a thing.

CHARMAINE: Not work.

BANKER WONG: No.

CHARMAINE: Not boy?

BANKER WONG: No. Not men, I'm . . . Never mind. No time.

CHARMAINE: Okay, not family?

BANKER WONG: No!

CHARMAINE: Not money!

BANKER WONG: NO!

CHARMAINE: What thing . . . ? What thing?

Beat.

BANKER WONG: . . . Why me? . . . I work out . . . I eat healthy.

. . . I quit smoking . . .

After a while:

CHARMAINE: Maybe you should start smoking again.

BANKER WONG *laughs. Really laughs.*

Feel better, okay? Want smoke? I have!?

BANKER WONG: No, no, I'm all right.

CHARMAINE: You come in then. You want some soup? It's good soup that I make myself. Good for you.

BANKER WONG: Soup is not going to help me . . .

CHARMAINE: Why not? It's good soup!

BANKER WONG: I don't want any soup.

CHARMAINE: You come in . . . no more run for today. You need soup.

BANKER WONG: I said NO.

CHARMAINE: No, you NEED to drink soup . . .

BANKER WONG: No, all right! NO!

CHARMAINE: But—

BANKER WONG: NO FUCKING SOUP!! What don't you understand?

Beat.

CHARMAINE: You going to pay me, then?

BANKER WONG: What?

CHARMAINE: PAY me for the massage!

BANKER WONG: Are you kidding me? What?

CHARMAINE: I give massage!

BANKER WONG: So?

CHARMAINE: Pay me!

BANKER WONG: Get lost!

BANKER WONG runs off.

CHARMAINE: *(yelling after her)* Who is going to fucking pay, eh? Who is going to fucking pay?

Scene 7: Penthouse

Early in the morning. PENNY *is repairing/sewing her very expensive underwear and bra set. She is in normal clothes, no makeup. She's quieter than we have ever seen her.*

PENNY: They never really buy you the right size, right?

Even if it doesn't fit, you put it on anyways. Prance round. But then, like, it's been worn, and then you an't exchange it for the right size. Trust me, I've tried.

They're usually too small. Those sales bitches probably say, "Is your friend petieeeeeeeeeeeete[5] like me?" And the guy gets hard and buys whatever they put in front of them. I mean, I get it. Everyone's gotta sell something.

But. But it means I gotta wear lingerie that doesn't fit! Or buy the same whole new set in my size? He's gonna wanna see me in it. Ugh, pisses me off.

My mom, my mom was tiny. She was perfect. Sometimes, she would say, "Penny, look at my waist. Aren't you lucky that having you didn't ruin my waist?"

This is an old set from a long time ago. I don't have anything else this nice. This is like, it's like recycling … I'm doing my part for the planet …

She continues sewing.

---

5 Petite.

I thought maybe at one time I could do fashion. Like I could design and stuff, I dunno. I dunno how you start to do something like that ... I guess you have to be smart, smarter than me anyway ... at least finish school. It's probably too late.

My mother had one good set too. I remember it, finding it after[6] ... All the little repairs on it ... You probably only ever really need one good set of lingerie. I mean, actually, they don't really notice it in the end.

There! I think it will fit again. Fingers crossed.

She gets dressed.

6 After her mother died.

Scene 8: Bank Conference Room

BANKER WONG addresses the assembled women. Very early in the morning.

BANKER WONG: Good morning, girls. Welcome to the Sunrise Club. This program is for winners only. Survivors. By the end of this quarter, there will only be half of you standing. By next quarter, less than ten percent. When I'm finished with you, I will recommend three of you for promotion into executive level positions. Last year, I only recommended two. One woman went to a competitor and leveraged herself more money.

The other woman thought she was going to replace me, but guess what, easier said than done. *(little laugh)* I think she raises goats now.

Who will you be? Survivor, or goat farmer?

Once you're in, you're in until I cut you. If that's not for you, if you like goats or llamas, if you just want a nice job, if you want a bit more work/life "balance," if you want to do good in the world—well, there's the door. Cut the bullshit and save us all the grief.

She waits, surveying.

No one? Good. Good. Really good.

She takes a deep breath, savouring it.

Ladies, let's learn how to make money.

Scene 9: Casino—Day

DEALER LI is at her table, fiddling with her cards. PENNY is uncharacteristically visiting the blackjack table in the daytime.

DEALER LI: You're not usually here this time of day.

PENNY: So what if I am?

DEALER LI: Nothing.

PENNY: Is the waiter gonna come around or what?

DEALER LI: Yah, he's coming. Shift just started.

PENNY: Hit me again.

DEALER LI: Are you sure?

PENNY: What did I say?

DEALER LI: Okay.

She busts out.

PENNY: Fuck! FUCK! Well, fuck you then!

PENNY leaves in a flurry, having lost a hand and not getting a drink. Her life is a series of these small conflicts. Nothing fits, nothing works, nothing goes her way. DEALER LI continues with her cards, an everyday occurrence.

DEALER LI: What a way to start the day, eh? I usually love a morning shift. But, yah, not usually how I like to start a double, with someone swearing at me.

That girl, I forgot her name, she used to come in with Frankie Pan. That guy, yeah. They call him Frankie the Rat, and worse names too ... Anyway, she'd come with these big parties of people looking for a good time. Back then, she might play a bit of slots, throw back some shots, and giggle as the coins came rolling out. She was the life of the party. You could see why she used to be on TV and stuff.

Look. Whatever. They sit, I deal. They bet, I collect. Most of the time, they lose. Sometimes they win. Sometimes that girl won. Not today.

She shakes her head.

In their heads, the last win is all that they can remember. They don't remember all the times they didn't win. All the money they lost. They just remember the fun parts.

I'm not judging. I used to be like her, the girlfriend, hanging off a guy's arm as he played blackjack. Not fancy like her, but y'know. Before I worked here, I was a cleaner in a hotel. I quit, because, well ... You see things, in a hotel ... Anyway, for a bit of glamour, I used to come here with my guy. At first, it was fun for us.

But ... it got away from him.

...

The thing is, our jobs, our jobs were okay, y'know, for jobs. We never really had a lot, but enough.

I'd work nights, he'd work days—six days on and two days off. And then we'd switch. Meant there was always someone there for the kids. Meant we could always have breakfast together no matter what. No matter how early it had to be, we would always sit down around the table. Sometimes he'd make Mickey Mouse pancakes and we'd daydream about saving enough to take the kids to Disneyland…

…

I don't know which came first. The factory looking around, seeing who they could get rid of, or my husband spending more and more time here at the tables. Here, without me, you know what I mean?

After, he was fired…he would say he was out looking for a new job, but I knew, I knew, he was coming here. Every once in a while he'd come home with a bit of a bounce and a handful of cash … I, just, I guess I knew but I was in denial.

Couldn't take it in the end, all his gambling. All the lies. So many lies. Packed the kids up, and off to my mom's. What else could I do?

That's when he really went downhill. I guess we were some kind of anchor, even if it didn't seem like there was anything left…

But I don't blame myself, all right? I don't. People, people make their own choices.

Beat. She fiddles with the cards, a distraction.

The kids, they don't know how he died, not really. I mean, I don't know how to explain it. They're older now, they might start asking questions. I worry, for sure. Man, do I worry about them, especially the eldest—

she's such a flighty thing. A pretty thing. Growing up so fast. And I'm working late all the time. I caught her wearing—oh my gawd.

It was something like that girl would wear. *(remembering)* Her name was Lulu! I mean, what was she even doing here so early?

That look when she sat down at the table ... I hate that look.

I would see that look in my husband's eyes when he was heading off to the casino...

That look. It's not about winning. It's not about fun.
That look, that hardness, it means she needs the money. She needs a lot of it, and she needs it bad. I mean, she looks rich, she dresses rich...

But I guess rich people need money too—more shit to pay for.

Scene 10: Casino Lobby

PENNY is in a state, pacing, fumbling with her purse. Perhaps waiting for a car.

PENNY: *(on the phone)* I'm sorry I'm late, Auntie . . . I know, I-I just have things to deal with, y'know? Just some bills, I mean, maybe we could talk about it . . . No, no, no, no, I don't mean a loan. No, no, I didn't mean that.

PENNY is disappointed.

I'll be right there, 'kay?
You know our lunches mean everything in the world to me!

Scene 11: Massage Parlour

CHARMAINE is chopping vegetables. SHERRY enters and CHARMAINE serves her soup. SHERRY places the fascinator in front of her. CHARMAINE can speak in any Asian language if desired, or in English.

CHARMAINE: This is nice. | This so nice.

SHERRY drinks her soup.

Where did you get this? | Where you get this thing?

SHERRY drinks her soup.

Did someone give it to you? | Someone give to you?

SHERRY drinks her soup.

Shrimp, you hear me?

SHERRY drinks her soup.

(a shift) Your mother sent a letter. | Your mother write letter.

SHERRY pauses but doesn't look up.

She hopes you are enjoying business college. | She think you enjoy business college.

SHERRY drinks her soup.

What did we say you are studying? | We say you study what class?

Beat.

SHERRY: Marketing.

CHARMAINE reaches across the table quite suddenly and violently.

CHARMAINE: Where did you get it? | Where you get this?

A flurry, a fight, a fascinator.

Scene 12: Dim Sum Restaurant

PENNY: *You're not my mother. You know that, right?*
I don't need your nagging!

AUNTIE KU is at a table alone. She is fussing with the tablecloth. There was a spill. PENNY has just left.

AUNTIE KU: So much drama with that girl! No matter, just a bit of tea on the table, it's fine, it's fine. My gawd, that girl, every day it's something else . . . I can't get a moment's peace!

She picks at her food or checks her phone.

I like this place. Old school, carts. Carts are great. Don't even need to stop eating. Don't even need to put your chopsticks down. Just wave at them with your mouth full, and voila, dumplings on the table.

There was a time my phone would ring non-stop, back in the day. Life of an entertainer—it was fun, fun for the young. Of course, I had the personality, and, believe it or not, I had the beauty too. Don't say, I know you want to say "you look great, you don't look a day past forty," but I know, I know. Trust me, I know what people say . . .

She texts.

I'm texting my boy. Maybe he'll join me. I hate eating dim sum alone! I will not eat alone. I refuse.

Hubert's my man friend—he is just so delicious. Yum yum yum. He's younger, of course. By a lot. More than whatever you're thinking. I don't know why it is such a big deal for people. No one would care if an older man dated a younger woman. No one would bat an eye!

PENNY: *It's completely embarrassing how you throw yourself at him!*

AUNTIE KU: That's what we were fighting about. She doesn't like Hubert, thinks he's taking advantage. And I don't like that Frankie Pan, because, well . . .

I'd take a Hubert over a Frankie Pan any day . . . Rather be with someone you can control, you know?

I just bought Hubert the sleekest, tightest little suit! So sleek. My goodness, they wear them tight these days. The tighter it is, the more fun it is to pull it off of him. Don't look so shocked. Did you think I was dating him for his brains?

I have expensive tastes, but Hubert, he? He has really expensive tastes. It adds up. Hubert is a good man, he could be out there working, doing something. I'm not saying he has to be rich, but he could at least try to make some money. I told him he has to get a job. That's why I bought him the suit.

PENNY: *He's just taking advantage of you! Why can't you see that!*

AUNTIE KU: It's true, I pay for everything. But how dare Lulu throw that in my face! It's not like she ever offers to pay for dim sum!

I hate fighting. I really do. My heart is so soft, soft as . . . *(she looks around)* Tell me if you see any mango pudding, 'kay?

Fighting—I can't take it, all the drama, the shouting, and carrying on.

Embarrassing. I mean, I eat here all the time. This is my restaurant. This is my table.

It really is my restaurant, in case you were wondering. Got my hand in a few things. Just in case. "Diversify" says Vivian. That's my banker. What a doll…

Life is easier with a bit more money, that's the truth. Don't let anyone tell you different. I have a lot of money. My husband (god rest his soul) worked hard—oh dear, the dear worked so hard. The hardest working man I ever knew. And he left it to me. I wouldn't want to disappoint him, bless him. Oh I had to learn. I always thought myself not too bright, but when I had to, I learned.

Just lucky me, lucky me. Lucky I had love. So I only had it once, but I had it, and I'm here alive because of it. And Lulu, oh, I don't know. She's been through so much … So many men, she should choose a nice one and settle down… Even if she doesn't love him… why not?

Did I love my husband? No, not at first, no! Of course not! I loved his money. I'm not ashamed to admit it. But the thing is, I love him now, that's for sure. I do.

Money is ridiculous, isn't it? It gets in the way of everything, it's everywhere. It can save a life or ruin it all in the same breath.

I hate it sometimes, even though it loves me.

Her phone rings and she answers.

Frankie? Is everything all right?

Whaaat?!

Scene 13: Head Bank Branch, Vancouver

BANKER WONG: So she knows Crazy Ku. So what? It really doesn't matter that she knows her, you know? That's not how it works, that's not how business is done in Canada. I may be Chinese, and maybe when we meet, we speak in Cantonese or Mandarin, it doesn't mean anything. We can speak in Japanese or French for that matter—still doesn't mean a thing. It doesn't mean we have an instant connection or history. It doesn't work that way. "Maybe we came from the same village..." Let's be clear: my family didn't come from a village. And people, Chinese people, they have some entitlement, let me tell you. No one is entitled to anything. Not money, not a loan, not a step up, not a kiss, not a job, and not anything.

And this little pageant lollipop shows up at my door...

PENNY: *We met before. My Auntie Ku introduced us... remember? So great to see you again!*

BANKER WONG: Amazing. Little bitch.

Beat.

The bank thinks I have a problem with women, but it's just not true. They give me male assistants now. Truth is, they're equally useless. No, my problem is—actually, my therapist says not to use the word "problem" but "challenge." Okay, my challenge is women like her. Not women in general.

Back when I started there were hardly any executives who were women. I set up a program for our female employees to have an opportunity to connect, network, share ideas and GET. AHEAD. The biggest thing, biggest obstacle for women? They get sidetracked, distracted by someone else's project, or doing their co-workers' work because they think they can do it better. Stupid. My advice—let your co-workers (MEN MOSTLY) deal with their own shit. Let them flop about and eventually fall flat on their face. Let them fail, I say. And then, when the dust clears, you can step in. And they'll welcome you. Trust me, everyone will be so happy to see you standing, they forget for a second that you're a woman. And that you're not white. But there you are. Here I am.

But you know, these mentorship programs are for women with potential, you understand? We empower hundreds of women. Not just any young woman. Not just any little piece of lipstick off the street. You don't want to throw good coins down a dark well. No one gets anywhere relying on chance, or luck, or fortune. No way.

Hard work. Brains. And knowing how to say "no."
No.
What I really wanted to say to her, to this Lulu girl:

Maybe you don't have what it takes to make it.
Maybe you don't deserve to make it in this world.

I've seen her, on TV, of course. On those shows. Hosting. She used to be on TV quite a bit, but I think she's pretty much relegated to being a pretty girl holding signs. No better than a signpost. The signpost is probably better value for the long-run, truth be told.

I actually saw her once, holding a sign, "hosting" at a marathon. Which one was it? Seattle? No, must have been here in Vancouver. Actually, my bank sponsors that one, so that's the first one I ran. It was for AIDS research. Boy that was a long time ago. When I used to run marathons in my spare time. Before, before[7] … Now, I run because … keeps me sane. Keeps me . . . busy. Chicago Challenge. Breast cancer, Toronto: Race for the Cure. Conquer Cancer, Calgary. Um, fight pancreatic, Ottawa. Ovarian, Chicago again. Yah, that's just all this year. In all, I think in the last three years of running, I've probably, by myself, raised more than four million dollars for cancer research.

Runs in my family.

I mean … well … not the marathons …

She is quiet for a bit.

What people don't realize is that being a top executive isn't just about the way we manage staff or bring revenue to the bank. The most important trait is how we actually take bad news. A real executive can take it. I can take it. I can take it calmly, looking right in your eyes.

Survivor.

A phone alarm goes off. BANKER WONG *takes out her pills, struggling slightly to open the bottle, and finally slamming it down.*

(*quietly*) Fuck.

She picks up the bottle again, opens it, and takes her pill in one smooth, confident swoop, following it up with water. She's embarrassed by her need for them.

So, you know, the nerve of this girl to show up at my door! Again! This

7 The diagnosis.

nothing with a counterfeit purse sitting in my office—I don't know where on earth she got that ludicrous purse. She probably thought it might impress me. A handbag, really? I'd use a bag like that to take a shit in.

She starts to smile a bit from the ridiculous memory of the girl's clothes.

Okay. Get this? The girl was wearing some sort of one-piece, like in pinstripe? A vest and thingy all attached. Not a suit, not a skirt . . . a romper, I guess!

She tries to contain her laughter.

I have never even seen such a thing before! A one-piece in pinstripe! A pinstripe onesie! I suppose she thought that was a serious outfit, oh dear. No, no, no, honey, you do not look like you could work in a bank!

She's still laughing.

Did she have a resumé?
Did she have any experience?
Did she even know what she could do in a bank?

No, we could not give her a "job."

Oh, she cried! Sure, she cried and cried. I gave her some tissue, told her her mascara was running, and sent her on her way.

I mean, I don't know how she got into this mess, but I'm sure as hell not fixing it. At least she didn't bring her modelling book this time!

She starts to giggle again.

A pinstripe onesie!

PENNY begs from behind a big desk.

PENNY: *But you could train me. I'll work hard, I promise! I'll work in the mail-room, please, anything…*

Scene 14: Casino

DEALER LI is waiting in a room at the casino. She's holding a five dollar chip.

DEALER LI: What the fuck. I mean . . . fuck.
I mean, I mean what the heck was I supposed to do?
This fucking job, I'm supposed to put up with that shit?
Seriously, that Frankie Pan is such a lying piece of scum. They got cameras everywhere, they'll look, they'll see. I did nothing wrong. I didn't touch him or anything. I shut the table, that's it.

Where are they? If they're going to fire me just freaking fire me already! Geez, you work at a place for years, you'd think they'd take your word over a rat. What the fuck.

Frankie today, he's in some shit mood, swearing and being rude. Shit mood cuz some deal, some deal went down. He's like, "My freaking condos!" and I just nod my head, uh huh. I don't care. I really don't care. I only care because if he is in too shitty a mood, he won't gamble.
So, anyway, Frankie was losing, losing bad. He swears at me. I've heard that language before, doesn't faze me! But then, he says, "Bitch, you're bad luck." I'm bad luck, okay, what the fuck. I've heard worse language, believe you me. I guess I made a face or something because he reacts. He gets this look, like what? And get this, the piece of shit doesn't flip a chip: he fucking throws a chip, a goddammed five dollar chip at my fucking head. So I shut down the table. I shut it down and I walked away. And if they are gonna fire me for that? So what.

I mean . . . Fuck . . .

She waits.

It was a mistake to even start working here. I don't know what I was thinking . . . The playing, the winning, it makes it feel like a party, people are so happy when they win. And, you know, people come here to be happy.

As the dealer . . . The thing about the chips, y'know? You handle them all day long. Some nights, some late nights, some long nights, I get staring at them and everything loses all meaning.

The chips, they're plastic. The money in your wallet, it's just paper. Coins, they're metal, but worth the least. A credit card—it's not even real. Just a computer keeping track. It's not real. These chips, money, none of it. It's not real, like who gives a shit! I don't give a shit.

A long beat, waiting.

Geez, fuck. I better not lose this job.

Scene 15: A Glitzy Store

PENNY, directly from her meeting with BANKER WONG, is still in her one-piece pantsuit. She is in an expensive store, holding some expensive clothing.

PENNY: You see me here all the time, right?

So why would I steal it?

Look at me, I mean, do I look like I need to steal it? I want to buy it.

So, just run it through then!

Oh my gawd. I don't know why you are making such a big deal.

What did I say? Didn't I just say that I'm buying it? Like, what's the problem? I gave you my card already!

THANK YOU.

...

(turning to another person in line) How hard is it to be a shop girl? Like how useless do you have to be to work in a shop?

No, no, you must be wrong. I have plenty of credit. I don't know if you know Tawny Ku but...

...

Can you just try it again?

Ridiculous.

(giving another card) Fine, try this one then! | Fine, try these then!

. . .

Oh my gawd, you know what?

(voice rising) This is bullshit. This is a bullshit store, with fake goods made in China. They don't know how to treat a customer, like at all! I don't know about you, but I'm taking my business elsewhere!

She storms out.

Scene 16: Massage Parlour

CHARMAINE is making soup nervously.

CHARMAINE: The Shrimp, she beg, she beg me, she no want to do.

What can I do?

This is work. All work like this.

The girl is lucky. Bigger man, richer man, mean bigger share, we richer.

Make the money, that's all.

Some men okay, some rougher, it's the same.

Work. Pay money. Do job. The way it is.

…

I start the same as her, as the Shrimp…

She will be okay. She will cry, all the girls cry so much. It's okay, it's okay, I say. Have some soup. They say thank you, Auntie, thank you, Auntie. Okay, I say, okay, quiet now, drink your soup. Shhhhh…
They cry in their soup, but they feel better.

…

I make soup, what can I do?

This is how it works.

Scene 17: Auntie Ku's Penthouse

Rain. It starts off quite light and builds in intensity throughout the scene.

AUNTIE KU opens the door.

PENNY: Omigod, omigod, omigod!

AUNTIE KU: Just . . . stop, for a second.

PENNY: I went to find you at mah-jong and oh my gawd you weren't there, and I was like, where is she? Where is she? And they wouldn't say—they wouldn't look at me! Why won't they look at me? I mean, those bitches—

AUNTIE KU: My friends. You mean my friends!

PENNY: I know but you weren't there, Auntie!

AUNTIE KU: Just stop for a sec—

PENNY: You're always at mah-jong—you're always there, like regular, where were you . . .

AUNTIE KU: Calm down—

PENNY: And I thought—I started to panic, imagining the worst, right? Like the worst things that could happen. Did you fall? Did you get in a car accident? Did a business deal go bad and they got to you?

AUNTIE KU: What kind of business do you think I do?

PENNY: Those bitches wouldn't tell me anything! They just looked at me, like I was a . . . like I was a . . .

Beat.

AUNTIE KU: What are you doing here?

PENNY *looks past* AUNTIE KU.

PENNY: What's happened? What's going on?

AUNTIE KU: Now is not a good time.

PENNY: Are you packing?

AUNTIE KU: You can't come in right now, Penny.

PENNY: Where you going?

AUNTIE KU: What do you want, Penny?

PENNY: I just . . . I just . . . wanted to see you.

AUNTIE KU: Do you want money? Is it money? Is that what you want?

PENNY: I, I thought . . . I'm sorry. I'm sorry.
That's what I wanted to say. For the fight, this morning.

AUNTIE KU: . . . That's it?

PENNY: Yeah.

Beat.

AUNTIE KU: I can't believe you. I can't believe you have the gall to come here.

PENNY: No, Auntie, I mean it this time.

AUNTIE KU: Do you? You mean it? Mean what?

PENNY: I'm sorry.

AUNTIE KU: Why are you sorry.

PENNY: I don't know why—I can't—what do you want me to say? I really mean it.

AUNTIE KU: Did you mean it when you said you would stop going to the club? Did you mean it when you didn't show up for that job interview? Did you mean it when you disappeared to Mexico for a month, and I only knew you were alive because of the charges on my card? I mean, I presumed you were alive. You couldn't bother to call to tell me.

PENNY: That was such a bad time. You know why…

AUNTIE KU: Okay, okay. But…but why now? Why can't you get yourself together?

PENNY: Auntie…

AUNTIE KU: I'm listening!

PENNY: Okay, okay. I can't . . . I can't . . . I don't know.

AUNTIE KU: You don't know why?

PENNY: I don't know why I do these things . . .
I'm just, I . . . I'm just . . .

I'm a fuck-up, okay. Is that what you want me to say?
I'm fucked up.
What am I supposed to do?
What do you want me to do about it?

AUNTIE KU: FIGURE IT OUT.

PENNY: Auntieeeeee . . .
I need you. I need help, I know. Help me.

AUNTIE KU: What do you think I have been trying to do?

PENNY: I know, I know, please . . .

AUNTIE KU: At some point you have to figure it out on your own. At some point you have to fight on your own!

PENNY: I know—

AUNTIE KU: At some point you have to want it to be better—

PENNY: I do—

AUNTIE KU: —but I keep seeing the same old shit from you!

PENNY: I try though, I do try—

AUNTIE KU: Do you?

PENNY: Yes, yes, I mean, I tried to get a job, but . . .
Like I don't know what to say, okay . . .

AUNTIE KU: Oh please. It's not about fucking up, all right, Penny? Fucking up I can deal with.

PENNY: I know I'm a fuck-up.

AUNTIE KU: I was a fuck-up too. But the difference between you and me? You, you, WANT to be fucked up.

PENNY: No, no, I, I, I . . . I'm trying . . .

AUNTIE KU: Penny. PENNY.

No. No more.

The condos? The deal fell through. It's over. Finished.

PENNY: Oh . . .

AUNTIE KU: Have you talked to Pan, that piece of shit?

PENNY: What about him?

AUNTIE KU: Why don't you talk to him first? He's probably got a few surprises for you. Go on, give him a ring.

Beat.

Call him! Give him a ring right now!

We'll see if he even takes your call.

PENNY: But … what … is it. How much did you lose?

AUNTIE KU: Do you care? Do you even understand? Do you even have a sense of anything beyond your own pretty face?

You want to know how much? A lot, Penny. A lot. I'm selling.

I have to sell, sell something, or I'll go under.

PENNY: Your condo?

AUNTIE KU: The condo building.
This building, and the one across the street, and the twin ones around the corner. I'm selling it all.

Beat.

Don't. Don't even try …

Y'know what? You know what, Penny?

It doesn't actually matter. It's not the money.
That's just … things.
What do you need with things, in the end? Really?

PENNY: …

The apartment is in shambles. PENNY *now really takes it in.*

AUNTIE KU: Hubert is . . . Hubert . . . left.

Not before grabbing everything worth anything in this apartment . . . just things . . . but . . .

Did I really think he would stick around?

Stupid of me, I know. I felt myself falling. I knew. I thought, here is this man. This man fits in my life. Or so I believed. I knew that I was falling, out of control, falling from a skyscraper, and I could've stopped, I should've stopped.

You need to stop, Penny. You need to stop, or you'll end up falling.

PENNY: Auntie . . . I'm so sorry.

AUNTIE KU: I called her . . .

PENNY: . . . Who?

AUNTIE KU: My daughter.

PENNY: Oh.

AUNTIE KU: Yah, I called her finally.

All along . . . what was I doing . . . ?

My daughter . . . my real daughter, Penny.

PENNY: Yah, I mean ... of course ...

AUNTIE KU: What's my daughter's name? What's her name? Do you even know?

PENNY: Is it, is it ... ?

AUNTIE KU: You don't know. All these years, all I did for you, you can't remember the most important thing about me.

You really don't know? Take a guess.

PENNY: ... I don't know.

AUNTIE KU: Grace. Her name is Grace.

Her father gave her that name. It was so important to him ... to name a child after something you can really believe in, and then that child would always be okay ... Her name is Grace.

Beat.

So I phone her. "Gracie, it's me." She answers, says hello, "Hello, Mummy."
Like she was little again ... my little girl ...

I heard her voice and ...

And that's it, and I knew, I knew she had forgiven me. Just like that.

It was just a wedding ...

A party, really! It's not like they had it in a church, or with a minister. Why wasn't I there? Why wasn't I there for her? Why didn't I just get on a goddammed plane and put on a dress…
But no…

I wasted so much time … so much time … because what?

I'm not young…
I'm not young.

Who is going to take care of me when I'm dying, Penny? You?

She looks at PENNY.

No, it's been too long, but maybe I'm not too late…
I'm missing it.
I'm missing her life.
I miss her.

I'm going to go live in Toronto. She even said I could live with her. I'm not ready for that … to live with her and her … wife.

Her wife's name is … Elisha. She's from Jamaica … and … and I don't know her at all yet. She seems … nice.

They have a son.

I never told you that. Cuz I didn't want you to think I was old.

I've never even met my grandson. And he's already three. He looks beautiful from the pictures. His name is Ralph, like an old man's name. Isn't that funny?

I want to be a grandmother. I'm ready. I want to be old. I want to grow old. Slow down. There will be a time, Penny, you might not believe it, but you might want this . . . family, love, peace. I'm ready.

By the way, I've cancelled your cards. Don't call me, don't message me, don't look me up. Try to do something with your life. Try to get old.

The rain gets harder.

Scene 18: Penthouse

PENNY, subdued, is gathering clothes.

PENNY: *(leaving a message)* Hey, hi, Frankie, it's me . . . I've left a few messages. Call me. Call me back when you get a chance. Okay, um . . .

Bye, and talk to you soon.

PENNY fights a battle in a swirl of dresses and fabric and movement. A persistent wound gnaws at her being.

Scene 19: Massage Parlour

Rain. PENNY *has just left.*

CHARMAINE: That rich bitch.
She come here, why she come here? What she think?

The Shrimp went to her for help, I know. I know she saw her and asked her. To help her.

I told the Shrimp, it's no good. Rich bitch no good for help. They don't care.

Ask for help? No point. No fucking good, I say.

Beat.

Aw fuck, it's bad. It's pretty bad. Bad man, a mean man, the meanest.

Aw gawd.
Messed her up. Messed her up so bad.

Shit.

Shitshitshitshitshit.

I take her to the hospital. Shit.
What else could I do? What else could I have done, okay?

PENNY: *I wondered, maybe, she might like some of these? They're nice. They're too small for me now. They were expensive.*

CHARMAINE: What are you going to say? It's not like she's family or friend or anything. Just another little rich bitch. Who gives a shit. I told her, I told her exactly what happened. Okay, little bitch, you want to know, so I tell her, I tell her what happened to the Shrimp.

PENNY is in agony. She was too late.

And then. That bitch. Her face, her face was all broken, like I smashed it. Like I took my fist and smashed her fucking face. Aw gawd, I want to. I wanted, y'know? You come here, you come here to my business, my place of business, and what? What do you want to hear? What are you doing here? You want to feel better? You want to rescue this little girl from bad people like me? We do massage, like it says on the door. Just because you think massage something different don't make me the bad guy. Fuck you, you little bitch.

She laughs.

What story you want to hear?

You want to hear nice story? Good woman? Nice girl? What you think? You think that maybe she changed her mind and went home? Went back to Thailand or the Philippines? Okay, she changed her mind. She going back to school. Study business now. Get a job, send money to her family. Everything okay. She okay. Little girl, okay! You want that? That's what you would like, I know. I know. Trust me, I know that dream! A dream, you hear me?

I say to her, "You stupid bitch! What you think?"

Some dresses not going to change anything, okay? A little dress no good, doesn't cover up bruises! A fucking bit of lipstick not going to help! Who care about fucking lipstick when she beat up so bad she look like an animal! An animal, you hear me! And these high heels, these shoes? Used shoe, you want to give used shoe, you stupid bitch.[8] How much were these? And you want to give them to her? Stupid shit. Shoes are no good! No good to her, because the last guy fucked her so bad, she cannot fucking walk!

So, I told her to get the fuck out. Shit.

PENNY stands in the rain with her bundle of clothes.

8 "Used shoe" is a Chinese euphemism for a woman who gets around; a whore.

Scene 20: Penthouse

PENNY is at home, still clutching the clothes meant for SHERRY. It's late.

PENNY: Things changed.

That's what he said.

"What do you mean?" I said.

"My situation has changed," he said.

Beat.

He bought me this one.
I can't remember...
Or maybe this one from...
...I used to get tons of stuff, right?

She picks up a fancy dress. She rips it quite deliberately and dispassionately.

(subdued) There was this one shoot. One shoot... it kinda changed everything for me... After that I...

Fuck.

It was going to be great—very high-concept. Like neo-enviro cool. They were going to fly me out to the islands, off the coast, like to the real rainforests. Rainforests in Canada, did you know that? I didn't know that before. And there are these bears—they're white, like not weird white with red eyes, not like that but real white. Gorgeous. They're extinct or something. Wait, no not extinct. I mean, anyway, rare. That's the environment bit.

At first I thought I would actually get to shoot with the bears, but no. They add the bears in post. So I never even saw one. But they dress me up, leaves and fairies, and they are all white, white—just like spiderwebs, like rainbows, like bubbles, and petals floating on the wind. Light like clouds, and soft like sleep.

Just so so so beautiful, you know?

And I think, I think I could be the queen, the wife of the bear, waking up from hibernation, the sun rising, reflecting off my pure fur—that could be me, right?

And these are the things I think about while they take my picture.

Click click click click click click click.

The cameras are digital, but the flash still makes sounds.

Flash flash flash flash flash flash.

I am gorgeous. I was the forest. I was everything.

She rests a bit in this memory.

Then later. Way later, months and months later, the spread is coming out. And, truth, it was so exciting. I mean it is a big spread, a big deal. There's a party for the launch at a fancy hotel. There's a red carpet and everything. I reach the end of the line, and there is the magazine. I open it. There is a little teaser pic of me at the front—amazing—the spread is called BARE NAKED.

Like B-A-R-E, get it?

And then I look up. The pages from the spread are blown up and placed all over for everyone to see.

Beat.

It's a lot of photos.

A lot. And the bear, he's there. He's beautiful.

And the forest, they're rainforests. It's beautiful.

And me…

Beat.

Well, the thing of it is, is that the dresses…

All the dresses were white…

So I wasn't really wearing anything under, y'know…

And… every time the flash went, I guess…

Bare… right?

Get it?

I, I, I—

I mean sometimes you can see some of the dress—a fold there, or a bit of ruffle…

In all the pics… you can see everything…

We hear flashflashflashflashclickclickclickclickfuckfuckfuckfuck-fuckfuck.

And I'm trying to be cool, right? The party, everyone who is everyone is there, but I just want to cry. The thing is they must've known, the photographer, the magazine people… It's digital—they had a monitor. Every time they took a photo, they knew, they saw.

But I didn't think that until later…

So then, the photographer comes up to me at the party—like he is really hot, right? And he still is the hottest thing, famous. I mean, after all the rumours about him, no one cares because he still is an amazing photographer. He asks me what I think…

I was young. I'm shy, so he tells me about the photos, what he used, how beautiful the light is on my breasts in that shot, how here, looking at a reflection of me, what he thinks about me, what he would want to do to me, how sexy I make him feel…

I feel better about the photos because everyone, everyone loves them. They love him. So they love me.

Later, lots of champagne later, he says, "I'm having a small thing upstairs, just me and my real friends"… I'm so flattered. I kiss him. He slips his fingers into me, right there in front of everyone . . . It happened so fast, hand up on my thigh, and then . . . I saw a woman, an older model, she was watching us. I locked eyes with her but then she looked down, looked away . . . I thought she was jealous . . .

Maybe she knew . . .
Maybe it happened to her . . .

So, I go upstairs with him.
Upstairs, there was more champagne and other stuff, anything you wanted . . .
People were still talking about the photos . . .
So he says, "Lulu, show us your poses—come on!"
So I do . . .
And he says, "No, no, no, like in the pictures . . . you don't need the dress, come on!"

So, so, so . . . I take off my dress . . .

And . . .

And . . .

Long beat.

I don't know. I don't know what happened that night . . .
I was in the hotel room . . .
There were a lot of people, men . . .

And . . .

I remember . . .

I tried to leave, but some hands, a lot of hands pulled me back onto the bed…

So many hands…

Later I looked at my bruises, and I thought whose hands are these?

And…

I remember…

I couldn't find anything… not my clothes, my purse…

A maid from the hotel found me in the bathroom…
That's where I woke up, face down next to the toilet.
She asked me if I wanted to call the police.

Why would I want to call the police?

I was so ashamed.

Everyone would know…

I shouldn't have…

The maid, she put me in a hotel bathrobe and snuck me out the side, so I wouldn't have to walk through the lobby. She asked me, "Can I call your parents?" And I said no. She said, "If I was your mom, I would want to know."

Anyway, the taxi took me to Auntie Ku's…

Poor Auntie, she cried so hard that day…

Long beat.

What's worse. What's worse is the magazine paid me so much.

A lot of money. A lot. And then, after the "party," they paid me a "bonus." But then they never hired me again…

Beat.

What's worse still?

Today, today, I'd kill to do another shoot like that.

Scene 21: Massage Parlour

CHARMAINE is over a little fire.

CHARMAINE: Long time ago…
A girl, young girl, want to get away…
Have an idea…
She light a fire, all the sheets go fire.
So she can escape, you understand?

It burn, burn, burn.
Everything burn.
I grab, I grab, I grab anything I can.
I run.
Run away just a dream, you understand?
They catch her.
"You want fire? Okay, we give you fire, little Mouse!"[9]

She starts adding documents and clothing into the fire. We catch a glimpse of the old scars on her arm.

They call me Mouse.[10] No one use your real name, you understand? No one ask. No one care.

No one likes to lose girl. But okay, now what? Me, I know. I know my boss, he mad. He will get mad! Who is going to pay? Who is going to fucking pay for the girl?

---

9 Or Monkey.

10 As above.

Stupid girl. Think she can run. Think someone rescue her, do something and help her. No, they won't, okay? I tried, many times. I run many times. No one cares about us. No one sees us.

They come here, police come?
I say, I will say, no I don't know this girl. I don't know her. No one saw her. No one know who she is. She is no one. No papers, no name, nothing, no problem. We do massage, like it say on the door.

New girl will come, from somewhere . . . There is always new girl.
New girl all the time.

There is a heavy knock on the door.

Scene 22: Li & The Girl

The rain continues. SHERRY *is on a train platform. She is in a hospital gown and hospital-issued pyjamas. She is walking but moving slowly because of her injuries. She looks around, wavering, waiting.* DEALER LI *enters. She is on the phone and oblivious to* SHERRY. *(If possible,* DEALER LI*'s lines on the phone should be spoken in Mandarin or Cantonese.)*

DEALER LI: *(into phone)* Wait till I get home—

...

Stop hitting your sister!

SHERRY: No, no, no.

DEALER LI: Wha—?

SHERRY: You no here, okay? | You're not here, okay?

DEALER LI: No.

(into phone) I don't know, I have to go.

SHERRY: Please...

DEALER LI: Go away.

SHERRY: Please...

DEALER LI: *(into phone)* I have to go...

She hangs up.

(turning to SHERRY*)* I just lost my fucking job! I don't have anything.

Beat.

SHERRY: Please . . .

DEALER LI: Get lost!

SHERRY: Go, I tell you go. | Go. I told you go.

DEALER LI: Get away from me. I don't have anything, all right!

SHERRY: No, you go! You go!

DEALER LI: No way I'm missing the last train.

SHERRY: You go!

DEALER LI: No way.

SHERRY: You go, you go! You understand! | Do you understand!

DEALER LI: Stop pushing me!

SHERRY: No, you go!
You go, okay!!!!
You have to go!!!
You go go go go go GOGOGOGOGO GO!!!!

DEALER LI: *(after a beat)* Fuck off.

DEALER LI walks away and takes a seat on the platform bench.

SHERRY: *(almost inaudibly)* I am something…

DEALER LI: *(to herself)* They gotta clean this city up.

DEALER LI watches SHERRY and eventually goes back to her phone, texting or emailing.

Unsure of what to do, and yet determined, SHERRY eyes the time of the next train. She wanders close to the edge. DEALER LI notices and realizes her intention.

What are you doing? Hey.

SHERRY: You go. | Go.

DEALER LI: Don't do it. Whatever you're thinking. Don't.

SHERRY: I told you go, go away. | I told you to go, go away.

Beat. DEALER LI wanders a bit on the platform, but she keeps looking at SHERRY.

DEALER LI: Hey! HEY! Come on!

SHERRY doesn't look at her.

Fuck, I'm not going through this again, okay?

I did this once, before, and I am not doing it again…

Hey! You hear me!

SHERRY: You don't know.

DEALER LI: Fuck you, I know! I know. I really know.

It's messy.
It's probably painful, you understand?
It will HURT.

SHERRY: I hurt already.

DEALER LI: Trust me . . . trust me . . .
It's worse—worse what you leave behind . . .

SHERRY: No one miss me . . . | No one will miss me . . .

DEALER LI really seeing SHERRY's injuries and something inside cracks.

DEALER LI: What the hell happened to you? Holy shit.

SHERRY finally breaks down and her heart crumples as one does when someone is finally kind.

SHERRY: . . .

DEALER LI: Oh, honey . . .

SHERRY: I can no, no more. | No, no more.
No more I can do— | Can't do anymore—

DEALER LI: Okay, okay . . .

SHERRY: I no go back. | I can't go back.
I run, I have to run.
Because she tell hospital. | Because she tells hospital.
She my auntie. | She's my auntie.
No auntie, bad lady. | She's not my auntie. She's a bad lady.

DEALER LI: No auntie, what? | She's not your auntie, what?

SHERRY: No . . .

She with them. | She's with them.
They hurt me.
Sell me to man, to hurt me. | She sells me to men.
They hurt me bad.

You understand? | Do you understand?

DEALER LI: Jesus.

How old are you?

SHERRY: She come back, she will. | She will come back, she will.
So I run—I run.
I want to stop.
I cannot.

Help me.
You help me. | Will you help me?
Please.

DEALER LI: Okay, okay, okay.

. . .

What's your name?

SHERRY: Sherry.

DEALER LI: Hi, Sherry. I see you. It's gonna be okay.

For SHERRY, a relief, a release, safety, and the comfort of empathy at last.

Scene 23: Penthouse

Quiet. Up in the sky. PENNY *is in a much worse state—more drinking, more drugs. She's been crying.*

PENNY: Thing is ... I know people. I know a lot of people. Friendly people, sure. That's all that they are.

Can I count on them?

Can I call them when ... when ... I need someone. When I need help.

Who would you call if you needed a ride from the airport?

If, if, if you could no longer pay your bills?

When your mother dies?

Who did I call?

Quiet.

I went—I went to try and find that girl. I went to find her ... And ... The way they lived, everything worn thin, thin and yet so tidy. Tidy as all hell ... broke my heart. Tidy ... and ready for the next customer. I went—I wanted to ... I dunno. I thought—I thought I could help her ... To be helpful, like try ...
That's what I wanted to know ...

If I can ...
If I am still worth something ...

That I'm something.

Beat.

I didn't win that pageant. I never won. I never won anything.
I was just a runner-up.
Not Miss Sunrise, but Lady Sunrise.
A lady, not a miss.
That sounds old, like a spinster…
Who wants to be a spinster?

She goes for her phone. She hesitates, but finally scrolls to a number and dials. A male voice answers: "Hello? Who the fuck is this?" She hangs up right away.

Oh shit, shit, shit. Why did I do that?

She goes to the balcony and throws the phone down, watching it fall.

It's so weird, so high in the sky. It's beautiful, but maybe it isn't right. It isn't right. Only birds live up this high. To live so far away from the ground. It seems far. Far enough.

Beat.

Gawd, it's late. It must be so late. It must be so late it's early.

Is it?

(looking down) Is that the sun? So low in the sky… It can't be that late.

I miss sleep. The proper sleep, the proper kind where you get up and your brain is clear, and your eyes are clear. Not rolling over, with mascara everywhere and my hair a nest and no memory of the night before...

Sleep, sleep, yes. Sleep is good.

She fumbles for some pills.

I miss it.

I miss...

I miss...

I miss...

I missed my life, I think.

...I remember. I remember now.

Pennies aren't extinct, they're obsolete!

Obsolete.

But I have one, I do, somewhere ... I do ... Oh my god, I do!

She fumbles with her purse, dumping it out.

This bag, there's nothing in here ... fuck.

Nothing. Just a fucking lip gloss ... what?

Oh shit. That's it?

That's all? That's all there is…

Oh shit.

Shit shit shit shit shit shit shit shit shit shit.

…Just a bit of lip gloss.

It looks pretty, but it doesn't stick around.

She finally lets go of everything that hurts. The sun rises.

Epilogue

BANKER WONG is running on her usual route.

As she is running along, she sees something farther along on the sidewalk.

There is a crumpled pile of pink peach and limbs.

She stops short, not sure what it is.

BANKER WONG: Wha—? What the—?

She gets closer. Then gasps.

Oh no. Oh god.

Once she realizes it is a body, she backs up from it.

The audience never sees the body.

...

Her heart is open and she cannot take her eyes off of what was once a human being.

She fumbles for her phone and hastily dials 911. She is capable of action in an emergency.

Hello, hello...

Oh my god, something terrible…

I need some help…

I need help…

Please.

~ end of play ~

Acknowledgements

This play would not have been possible without the immense encouragement of Dr. Siyuan (Steven) Liu and John Cooper and UBC's commissioning and development support. This play has also received workshops and development support from the Banff Playwrights Lab, Cahoots Theatre, the Arts Club, and Factory Theatre, as well as additional funding from the Ontario Arts Council and the Wuchien Michael Than Foundation. Much gratitude for their support of this work, and new works in general!

I am so grateful to wonderful insights along the way that gave shape to this work, whether they were officially named dramaturgs or not: John Cooper, Eury Chang, Rachel Ditor, Veronique West, Jivesh Parasram, Brian Quirt, Jenna Rodgers, and Matt McGeachy.

Much gratitude to Nina Lee Aquino and the entire team at Factory Theatre for bringing the work to life and refining its form. In addition to the tremendous premiere cast and creative team, I am indebted to all the actors who participated and gave of themselves for workshops at the University of British Columbia, the Arts Club, Banff Playwrights Lab, Cahoots Theatre, and Factory Theatre.

So I wish to thank all the workshop performers (in alphabetical order):

Sara Canero, Lana Carillo, Shiong-En Chan, Jemmy Chen, Evelyn Chew, Ma-Anne Dionisio, Grace Fatkin, Carolyn Fe, Tracey Ferencz, Susanna Fournier, Cynthia Hicks, Josette Jorge, Stephanie Jung, Courtney Ch'ng Lancaster, Eileen Li, Jane Luk, Christine Nguyen, Laara Ong, PJ Prudat, Rosie Simon, Regina Simon Beecham, Valerie Sing-Turner, Pamela Sinha, Donna Soares, Angela Sun, Athena Kaitlin Trinh, Jean Yoon, and Amanda Zhou.

Marjorie Chan was born in Toronto to Hong Kong immigrants who arrived in the late '60s. As a theatre and opera artist, she works variously as a writer, director, and dramaturg, as well as in the intersection of these forms and roles. Her work has been seen and performed in the United States, Scotland, Hong Kong, Russia, and across Canada. Her full-length works as a playwright include the plays *The Madness of the Square, a nanking winter, Tails From the City*, as well as libretti for the operas *Sanctuary Song, The Lesson of Da Ji, M'dea Undone*, and, most recently, *The Monkiest King*. Some of the companies Marjorie has directed for include Gateway Theatre, Cahoots Theatre, Native Earth Performing Arts, Theatre Passe Muraille, Obsidian Theatre, and Theatre du Pif (Hong Kong). Marjorie has been nominated for nine Dora Mavor Moore Awards and won four. She has also received the K.M. Hunter Artist Award in Theatre, the My Entertainment World Award for Best New Work, and a Harold Award, as well as the George Luscombe Mentorship Award. Other notable nominations include the John Hirsch Director's Award, the Governor General's Literary Award for her playwriting debut, *China Doll*, and the Canadian Citizen Award for her work with Crossing Gibraltar, Cahoots Theatre's program for newcomers. She is also Artistic Director of Theatre Passe Muraille in Toronto.

First edition: June 2022
Printed and bound in Canada by Rapido Books, Montreal

Jacket design by Christine Mangosing

202-269 Richmond St. W.
Toronto, ON
M5V 1X1

416.703.0013
info@playwrightscanada.com
www.playwrightscanada.com
@playcanpress